Christmas Rhymes and Pantomimes

by Hazel Rennie

Published by Treewych
Hazel Rennie, 157 Lyndhurst Road,
Worthing, W Sussex, BN11 2DG

ISBN Number 978-0-9567247-0-0

Printed by:
Baker Press Ltd
Ferring, Worthing,
BN12 5JP

Other collections by Hazel Rennie:

- 'Poems and Rhymes for Children aged 3 yrs to 103 yrs'

- 'We Told You So' (War and Peace)

Contents

Pantomimes

Bringing Home the Yule

Hayley Davey

Bringing Home the Yule

A dad and his lad
　　　went over the snow
To bring home the Yule

The Yule log was dead
　　　felled long ago
Well weathered Yule

They roped it to drag
　　　with cheerful 'Heave Ho'
Welcome to Yule

Lasses are glad
　　　with ribbon and bow
Prettifying Yule

A charred piece to add
　　　and blessing bestow
To first flame Yule

Lasses and lads
　　　sing round the red glow
Three cheers Yule

'Remember,' says dad,
　　　'we save some you know
To light next Yule.'

Christmas Market

Have you been to the Christmas Market
when the dark falls early?
Lanterns, lamps, dropping pools of light,
golden, pearly.
When you go to a Christmas Market
on a tide of people not seen before,
jostling, pressing, surging - then suddenly,
the folk next door!

Oh, the smells from a Christmas Market,
promising rare pleasure,
pungent fumes breathing zest and spice,
taste and treasure!
Grills and fryers flame and sizzle,
launching waves of mouth-watering choice,
savoury, syrupy, sumptuous,
succumb, enjoy.

Christmas Market

Aladdin's cave, the Christmas Market,
stalls with goodies piling,
glittering bargains for you to buy,
rare, beguiling.
Toys and trinkets, silks and sparklies,
a joyous rush - all caution spent
stall to stall all bags filling,
well content!

When you leave the Christmas Market,
that special aura lingers
in the parcels opened by those eager
little fingers.
A traditional Christmas Market
noisy, busy, colourful displays,
remain a memory ever after.
Echoing simple, *happy* Christmas Days.

Christmas 80 Years Ago

A village in Yorkshire on the edge of the moors,
In little stone houses, uncarpeted floors,
Generations of families all lived within call,
Sharing high days, low days, celebrations and all.

Of all Seasons remembered Christmas was best
For fun, food, festivities and goodwill expressed.
Carolling, mumming, round all the doors,
Including the lonely ones out on the moors.

Round the Tree dressed in glory, her candles
alight,
We held hands and danced, eight steps left, eight
to right.
Hung up Uncle John's socks (with the biggest
feet!)
For Santa to fill with sweets, fruit and a novelty
treat.

Nobody'd tell tales to Santa of misdeeds or
disgrace,
So fell into untroubled sleep with a smile on our
face.
Next morning, curled up in broths of excitement
to wait
'Til we're told, 'Breakfast's ready, there's a good
fire in t' grate.'

Christmas 80 Years Ago

Drag on clothes, rush downstairs, quick as say
snap,
Crowding together to rinse hands at the water
tap.
While our plates of porridge are being dished out
Pull Santa's gifts from the socks with a yell and
a shout.

When the breakfast dishes were all cleared away,
Came the biggest excitement of Christmas Day.
Presents bought by Mum, Grandma, Uncle,
Auntie,
Were last night, from his sleigh, delivered by
Santa.

Exciting parcels piled on various chairs,
Rush round them to glance, 'Mine? or theirs?'
Bright paper, patterned with reindeer or holly,
Torn away to discover a game, a ball, or a dolly.

Aunt Lizzie raked the fire below the oven to roar,
Now and then opening the big black oven door,
When the Christmas dinner sent messages round,
'Soon be ready, nicely crisped and browned'

Christmas 80 Years Ago

Oh! Roast potatoes, parsnips and gravy soaked meat,
The green peas and sauces and every last treat.
A few glorious munching minutes made it all disappear,
Then 'Hurray for Christmas pudding!' welcomed each year.

Deliciously rich in pools of sauce, white and thick,
Tongues carefully probe for a silver three-penny bit.
Then we little piggies lean back from the trough
With glasses of fizzy lemonade to finish us off.

Then outside to play with our friends in the snow,
Sliding and making snowballs to throw,
Whizzing down hills, if you didn't have a sled
Went down on a kitchen shovel instead.

Evening - corned beef, celery, jellies, custard, cream,
And a Christmas Cake completed the dream.
Games, charades, a party piece to recite,
Carol singing, and then 'Goodnight.'

Us Mummers

Us Mummers are coming
Us Mummers are coming
We're coming a-mumming
We're coming a-mumming
We're coming a-mumming today.

We'll dance you a mime
Tell you a rhyme
Scrub yer stones
Click on t' bones
We only asket
A penny in t' basket
A pretty ring
Or any owd thing.

Us mummers are coming
Us mummers are coming
We're coming a-mumming
We're coming a-mumming
We-re coming a-mumming today.

'Let's Go Look at the Crib'

One afternoon during Christmas school holidays,
Ruby Weaver and Beryl Taylor went into the
village church to visit the Nativity there.
They squatted beside the wooden manger where,
wrapped in a soft white shawl, the doll lay on a
bed of straw. Ruby lifted the doll and unwrapped
it with care.
'I knew it!' she cried, 'They've left it all bare.
He'd have had a piece of cloth round his bum
at *least*. Mary wouldn't have used pampers, we
know *that*, but she would've covered his bum for
when he shat.'
Wrapping the doll in the shawl, Ruby replaced it
in the manger.
They turned to look at Mary, 'She looks old.'
said Beryl, 'She looks at least twenty three, but
Mary was a teenager, so we've allus been told.'
'That's right,' agreed Ruby, 'and I'll tell you
summat else, I smile to meself when I hear
'em reading out "Jesus was born and laid in a
manger" as if that's all there was to it! "Here he
is, plonk him in there." Mary was a young un,
but I can't see her doing that, just as me Mum
would've been off her head if she'd done that

wi' us. Well I reckon Parson knows no more than them that wrote about it. Too eager to tell about the star and kings and all the glory, if you ask me. If women'd had a chance, they'd have told a proper story, about Mary telling Joseph to fetch a bucket of hot water, to give the manger a good scrub out.'

'Have you noticed?' asked Beryl, 'There aren't any women visiting Mary, just kings and shepherds. Can you imagine women not visiting when there's a young 'un on her own? They'd have broken their necks to get there. Telling her what to do about this, and helping her with that. They'd have been bossing Joseph about and telling t' shepherds to get back a bit and keep their mucky paws off the manger. We know there'd be guardian angels around, but I can't see *them* knuckling down to cook her a meal. Anyway their wings'd get in t' way.'

Ruby grinned, 'Yes and there'd be a right stink of burnt feathers about the place.' and both of them cracked up.

Ruby turned to look at the kings, 'Hey, look at this, they look like real jewels in his crown and this one has a pure white linen cloth on his head, with a thick gold cord to hold it on. Looks dead smart.' She stood looking at the king for a moment, then turned, 'You know, Beryl, I can't make out them kings at all. They gave presents, one is a lump of gold. Now, can *you* picture Joseph going to book into one of the best hotels for a couple of weeks? People in charge might be more likely to hang on to the gold and chuck him out. Whereas if the *kings* had gone to book up *for* 'em, they'd all be bowin' and scrapin', offering the best of everything. But the kings didn't **do** that. They paid a visit, gave presents and went off, leaving 'em in the same grotty place they'd been in when they found 'em!' she waved her hands about, 'I bet Mary couldn't believe it! I bet she was looking out the rest of the day for the kings coming back to say, "We've booked somewhere comfortable for you, we'll take you there now." Well anybody *would* think that, wouldn't they?'

'And after that,' Beryl put in quietly, ''They became refugees, having to run to Egypt because Herod wanted to kill the baby.'

They looked at each other, 'Poor kid,' they said,
'she must have been scared out of her wits.'
Ruby reached out to give Mary a sympathetic pat
on the shoulder.
'They don't say how they got on in Egypt.'
mused Beryl, 'Refugees are sometimes treated
badly here, I hope people weren't unkind to
them. There's so much left out.' she said, 'I'm
going to see if there's a way of filling in the
blanks. You know, do some *research.* '
'We could ask Miss Grant in History,' suggested
Ruby.
'Yeh, that *is* a good idea.' replied Beryl, 'And
what if we write, "The Story According to
Mary"? I bet we'd have better ideas of it than
scribes and parsons.'
'Yeh,' said Ruby, 'We'd be making up, a bit, for
the rotten time she had.'
A final pat to the wool shawl, and they turned
towards the aisle,
'Bye Jesus, Bye Mary,'
Ruby adding, 'Bye Joseph, I reckon you were an
alright bloke.'

Christmas 1929

In my nightie, from the kitchen doorway,
I look into an unfamiliar place.
Glitter, greenery, bright red berries
festooning the picture rail to grace
a sepia troopship, returning
Uncle Harold from the Great War.
Roasty, spicy, fruity, unknown smells
from the kitchen range, evoking … Zanzibar?

I run to the centre table.
The biggest book ever seen,
a bird with a lady riding
on its back, or maybe a Queen.
'MOTHER GOOSE' golden letters shine.
They tell me the book is mine!

CHUKA!

A Winter's Tale

It was a cold, sharp night I remember. I was tired
and could find nowhere to rest, nowhere safe
even to linger.
I'd run away from my mistress. I'd tried to do all
she required,
it was never enough. She beat me. I was afraid
she'd send the bell ringer
to hound me out. I needed to get in somewhere to
hide.
Dodging from one shadowy place to the next and
praying,
'She must not find me - not find me - I need
somewhere to bide'.
I saw a wooden shack, the door seemed loose,
slightly swaying.
Easy for a small girl of ten to steal inside without
a sound.
I stood staring into the dark. A narrow
moonbeam slid down, lighting
animal shapes bedded down on the ground.
Then I heard snoring! People! I stood perfectly
still, fighting
to hold my breath from gasping. How long I
stood there

A Winter's Tale

I don't know. Everywhere remained quiet, apart
from the breathing
of animals, people, scenting and warming the air.
Then I saw something else. Holding me to stare,
disbelieving
my eyes! Must be the moonbeam across the dark,
a flaw
in my view of it - but no, I was not mistaken,
there was certainly a baby lying in the manger on
a bed of straw.
Carefully resting my hands on the side of the
manger so as not to waken
the sleeping bairn, I knelt to look more closely. I
felt so sorry,
these poor people, with a baby no more than a
few days old.
I'd nothing to fear from them, seemed they had
far more to worry
about than a kid coming in, seeking shelter from
the cold
I felt a movement behind me, a light touch on my
shoulder.
I spun round on my heels, looked up into
compassionate eyes

and buried my face in her skirt. She was young,
not much older

than I was, but I felt safe. If she had not helped
me to rise

I'd be there still! She folded a blanket round me
and laid

me gently down on straw soon drenched with my
thankful tears.

Stroking my brow, softly singing a lullaby, she
stayed

by my side until, soothed and freed from my
fears, I slept.

In the morning we got up early. Her husband was
there.

I helped them with the baby and everything.
They kept

me with them. We moved off quickly, I didn't
ask where

we were going, I knew they were afraid

but they never talked about it. They talked to me

asking me about myself. We travelled on. I
stayed

with them. I felt we were a family, we three

and the baby. One place, we were given supper

and bed for the night
by kindly people. Mary, taking my hand, after
breakfast the next day,
went to the lady and, holding my hand tightly,
told her I had need,
would she take me in? I stood very still and quiet
as the lady said 'Yes'.
I turned to Mary, putting my head on her
shoulder, but did not plead,
I trusted her and didn't want to cause her more
distress.
Before they left we stood in a tight circle,
wetting the baby with our tears.
I watched them walk away. Just before they
were out of sight
they turned, raising their hands to me. I've been
here, now, for *years*.
We often talk of them, those good people. I hope
they might
think of me sometimes. I've never moved away,
I'd be afraid
to leave just in case they returned and were
passing through.
That's my secret hope. I've been treated kindly

here so I've stayed.

I see them in my mind, smiling into my eyes as
they used to do,

and the baby! He'll be grown a fine, strong
young man, now,

nearly thirty years old! From his parents he will
receive

their calm compassion. He will be tall and
straight, a noble brow.

I can't *know*, of course, but that is what I believe.

He will be a good man … I am sure life will be
treating him kindly.

Mistletoe Magic

See where the mistletoe clings to the apple tree,
Take silver scissors sharp as a shark's tooth,
Snip the green tendrils and bring them home to
me,
With the white berries to tell me the truth.

Walk through the woodland, look for a hazel tree,
Test how the branches spring in your hands,
With a short sharp knife cut and bring home to
me
Two fine slender hazel tree wands.

Bend the wands into hoops, bind each with a
silken thread,
Slide one hoop inside the other athwart,
Within tie the mistletoe, hang the ball overhead.
Who passes beneath, with a kiss may be caught.

The kiss may be motherly, brotherly, but if a true
lover be,
The hazel boughs tremble, a white berry will fall.
I shall wait there, until he comes to lean over me,
With a kiss, to proclaim my love holds him in
thrall.

Stroppy Girl

*(Stroppy schoolgirl having a good old moan to herself
about Christmas)*

'It's the *thought* that counts'   They keep telling
me that.
Mum says 'You can't expect *all* your wants to be
satisfied.
You have to be thankful for what you're given,
and that's flat.
The presents people give is for *them* to decide.
Some things might be too expensive, you must
realise.
Or something you wanted, it might be the shops
have sold out.
Anyway, just accept each present as a lovely
surprise.
Remember, there are children everywhere having
to go without...'
                    Blah, blah, blah.
Well, *I* think some people choose presents just as
a wind-up.
I *mean,* sewing sets! colouring books ! From
ancient aunts.
And again, imagine somebody doddering about
trying to make their mind up

between a box of fancy hankies and warm winter
pants.
Or scenty cream to make your armpits smell of
lavender or *rose.*
Or those fiddly little bags holding tiny cakes of
soap!
Or bottles of other smelly stuff. Why don't they
ever sell out of those?
Never. They're in the shops *every* year, so there's
no hope.
Well, it's always been the same. Jesus was given
perfume and he's a boy!
And that was from wealthy kings! Imagine
somebody like them, top rank.
What a shame. They should have given him a
fantastic toy.
One of 'em gave him gold. Bet it was taken
off him, to put in the bank.
Bet he wasn't allowed to spend it … come to
think, it might all have been lost…
you know, when they had to leave in a hurry …
running away
from Herod … I wonder, would those be the
things they treasured most?

With my friends, we've sometimes asked each
other, 'What would you say,
is the *one thing* you'd grab, if you had to leave
five minutes from now,
and never come back? Nobody mentions
Christmas presents, that's for sure.
Actually it always takes us longer than five
minutes, because somehow,
we never remember what we said before -
anyway it was all a bore.
Nobody came up with anything near as mind
blowing
as a lump of gold! I do remember
when I was a little kid,
every present was exciting. Though one, had me
throwing
a fit. It frightened me so. Every time I looked at
it I ran away and hid.
It was a small skinny doll, and behind its neck
were two little sticks
that you pressed together, and its mouth shot
open to show
two rows of big teeth, gnashing sharp, snappy
Clicks.

Those teeth visited my dreams, dancing towards
me like a chorus row.
Yeah well, looking back at Christmas presents,
suppose I did alright.
But that was *then*. This is *now*. There's no fun
any more.
People give me clothes - they're either too big or
too tight.
Our Christmas party, they'll all be kids or
ancients, so *that'll* be a bore.
Yes I'm *grumpy*. Well, Christmas has caused me
to *think*.
There are so many things wrong, can't find the
words to explain.
When I thought about Jesus's family running
away, *that* was the link,
I wonder why do all the *horrible* things go on
happening again and again?
He was a refugee, wasn't he? and what's
happening today?
People running away because somebody's after
them, to capture or kill.
Ordinary families, some of them - just like mine.
You know, just thinking about that sends a chill

right up my spine.

Yeah, well, I know, I started out in a right bad mood,

moaning about Christmas presents, and what's in the shops.

Can't say I've cheered myself up, but reckon I've changed my attitude.

I have no reason for getting into a fit of the strops.

So-o? ... Nah, doesn't mean I'm growing wings

\- not an angel's anyway,

D'you reckon they might pass for the Christmas Tree Fairy?

I'll be doing my best, taking presents off the Tree and handing 'em out on Christmas Day,

with *big smiles for everyone*; hope they don't find that too **scary!**

First Foot

First Foot knocked on the door,
Came in with brush and shovel,
Swept fire back and front hearth floor,
Taking careful trouble.
Sweeping Old Year clean away
To welcome New Year in,
With traditional words to say
And ancient charm to spin.
'A lump of coal, a pinch of salt,
A piece of new baked bread,
Never a voice to be finding fault,
All Blessings for the year ahead.'

Miss MacRone's Christmas

They say Miss MacRone
lives all alone
and isn't looking for friends.
Lives in a shack
off the beaten track
and neither borrows nor lends.
Receives no gifts
when deep snow drifts,
not a crumb of Christmas cheer.
'She must be so sad,
or stark, staring mad'
that's what they say round here.
I'll whisper to you
that's not quite true,
because last Christmas I went to see
if Miss MacRone
was quite alone
I'd give her a card from me.
But when I spied
laughed 'til I cried
at the sight through her window there!
A cat played the fiddle,
Miss MacRone in the middle
of foxes and frogs, weasels and dogs, badgers

and
rabbits and hares.
She, dancing knees high,
spirited, spry,
with surely no troubles or cares.
A frog twanged a banjo
for foxes to tango,
and squirrels hopped about offering Christmas
cake.
Now you will see
and surely agree,
whatever wild tales the gossips may make,
Truth can be crazier, and if told with humour,
more beguiling, intriguing,
enchanting, inveigling,
     than boringly tedious, repetitive Rumour.

A cat played the fiddle...

Hayley Davey

Christmas at Sea

A Duck, a Cow and a Christmas Tree
Agreed to spend Christmas sailing the sea.
Made common sense
Would save on expense
Need cater for a party of no more than three.

Cow found a tin bath on the farm,
Remarked 'Though the seas be stormy or calm,
This bath made of tin
Will let no water in
You may step aboard with never a qualm'

Duck quacked 'Because I can swim
You may trust me with your life and limb.
First sign of attack
I'll turn round and swim back
To fetch coastguards from Westbury Trim.'

They launched their bath on Christmas Eve,
Such outrageous adventure no one would
believe,
Christmas Tree in the middle,
Cow sang 'Hey Diddle, Diddle'
'I name this bath,' quacked the Duck,
'Salty Steve'

They sang, played games, including charades,
Composed clever rhymes for their Christmas
Cards,
Sent greetings of cheer
To all ships far and near,
Morse-coding the messages on their guitars.

The Duck, the Cow, and the Christmas Tree,
Returned to the farm at the end of their spree.
The tale is told,
Of three sailors bold,
Renowned, in the annals of 'Christmas at Sea'

Hanging Christmas

Hang paper chains from wall to wall
Hang Christmas Cards for all to see
Hang the mistletoe in the hall
Hang the trimmings on the Tree.
Hang a Santa dressed in red
Hang out a welcome holly wreath
Hang a stocking by your bed
Hang a pillow case underneath.
Hang on to the 'Thought that counts'
Hang around with wealthy friends
Hang on while excitement mounts
Hang your hopes on dividends.
Hang in there as time goes quicker
Hang your heart out on your sleeve…
Grrrrrrrr… hang the turkey, hang the vicar,
Let it all hang out for what you DIDN'T
                                          RECEIVE!

A Christmas Fool

(with apologies to Rudyard Kipling)

If you can keep your head when all about you
Are losing theirs imbibing potent wine,
If you can trust yourself, though others doubt
you,
To say 'See my silken, silver, slippers softly
shine.'
If you can dance and not be tired by dancing,
Or playing games without a sigh or yawn,
Never noticing the hands advancing
Round the clock toward the break of dawn.
If you can laugh at all the jokes, be jolly, hearty,
Eat far more than your share of Christmas food,
And offer to make coffee for the party
While all other bums on chairs stay firmly glued.
If you can fill the odd embarrassing minute
With an anecdote or clever pun,
Then *yours* is the sink, and everything that's in it,
To wash up, - for *you* are the only sober one.

Carol Singers

Late afternoon and already dark;
'I vote we go carolling,' said Mark,
'there's somebody living in the Grange.
Been empty for ages, isn't it strange
moving in, and Christmas so near?
You'd think it'd take *months* to clear,
it must be in a right old state.'
We leaned, looking in through the gate,
A long, lonely, stretch of snow.
Small voice, 'I - I don't think I want to go.'
Jean took his hand, 'Come on Tommy love,
we're gonna sing carols, give the gate a shove.'
The drive stretched long and straight,
we ran, we skipped and pretended to skate.
All wearing clogs, didn't make much sound,
snow being crisp and thick on the ground.
'You sure somebody's living here?'
Gordon asked, 'if they are, seems kinda queer.'
The house showed not a glimmer of light,
all its windows shuttered tight.
We stood round the door, throats suddenly dry;
'OK' I said, 'Ding Dong Merrily on High'
it's cheerful, and we know it well,
sing a few lines then I'll ring the bell.'

Carol Singers

(I'm the oldest of our family you see
at times like this feel it's down to me).
No bell, a brass knocker, rise on my toes,
both hands grab for three heavy blows.
At first knock the door flung open wide,
we jumped back, 'Goblins!' little Tommy cried.
'Carollers! Come in, come in, one and all!'
Faces smiling kindly from the hall.
'Come, entertain our party!' they invite.
Into a crowded room, bright
with candles, lamps and a blazing fire,
tables laden with dishes, 'Whatever you
desire…'
Fruit, pastries, sweets never tasted before,
such welcome warmed us to the core.
We sang all the carols learned at school,
Gordon showed magic tricks, playing the fool;
Mark is a good mimic, but gave me a scare
when he aped some of the company there!
They didn't like that, I just *knew,*
and from then on my worries grew.
I got ready to say, 'We have to go,'
all the lights turned down low
and, from the blazing fire,

Carol Singers

flames leapt higher and higher,
shadows danced along the wall.
I couldn't see the kids at all.
Strange music then began to play,
loud and fast; someone whirled me away,
round the room in a crazy dance,
every now and then I caught a glance
of the others, being wildly swung about.
The music stopped. I quickly gave a shout,
'NOW WE'LL SHOW YOU OUR CLOG
DANCE!'
(That's how we always ended our performance.)
Jean had the gumption to recognise her cue,
'Come on kids you know what to do!'
We hopped and clogged to the end of the dance,
but to my horror, before I took my chance,
someone stood little Tom on a polished table top,
'Now little man, let us see *you* hop, hop.'
I leaned on the table very close to him, afraid
of an unknown danger into which we strayed.
On the shiny surface, Tom performed his dance,
beaming his delight being given his chance.
Then I lifted him down and held him tight,
'We must go now, thank you. Goodnight.'

I looked at their faces with a chill of fear,
nothing was left of their good cheer.
Then one stepped forward, 'Her name is Irene,
the children may go with Peace, serene.'
They stood in silence as he took us to the door.
I hurried us out into the night, before
they changed their minds, and took us back.
As we retraced our steps down the snowy track
we were silent. Then Gordon spoke,
'We'd better not tell anybody about them folk.'
'And **don't,**' I said, 'any of you **dare** to drop
a word to Mum, about that polished table top
Tom clog-danced on. She'd be *that* shocked.'
'That wasn't our fault. Just that Mark mocked
them, then it all seemed to change.' replied Jean.
'And what,' chimed Gordon, 'was with *your*
name, Irene?'
I told him, 'Reckon he was telling them you
could go with me,
they accepted because Irene means Peace, y'see.'
'Funny house, funny folk, funny party. Not much
fun,
said Mark, 'If ever I go near the Grange I'll **run**!'
'I **said** they were Goblins,' remarked little Tom.

I told you they were goblins…

Hayley Davey

A Christmas Present (to present)

I have a Christmas present to present
but as she is not present at present
I shall present it presently
when she presents herself.
However the present heat,
presenting the present stuffy atmosphere
present in this room, may presently
present a problem.
The present is a Christmas cake.
The present icing design presented,
may, from the present atmosphere,
presently present a runny blob.
Presenting an ever present danger
that, when she presently presents herself,
I may be presented with the embarrassment
of presenting, not a present,
just a ghastly gooey mess - ugh!

Experience

I stepped out into a wonderful world of stardust,

I walked carefully over silver pointed edges of stars,

I ran, and the stardust leapt and ran by my side,

I stopped. The stardust fell and slowly, silently, settled.

I went back inside wearing a tingling, sparkling glow.

They laughed and said, 'Look at you, all covered in snow!'

A Christmas Child

Snowdrop Willoway,
Born on Christmas Day,
Shouted 'Hip Hooray!'
On her first birthday,
For the shiny falderay
All around the house; to say,
'This is Snowdrop's Birthday!'.

On her second birthday,
Snowdrop shouted, 'Hip Hooray,'
For the shiny falderay
Round *everybody's* house; to say,
'This is Snowdrop's Birthday!'

On her third birthday,
Snowdrop shouted 'Hip Hooray,'
For her toys from Santa's sleigh,
And all the shiny falderay
Round the shops in town; to say,
'This is Snowdrop's Birthday!'

On her fourth birthday,
Snowdrop shouted, 'Hey! Hey! Hey!
Everybody shares *my* day,
Share even the toys from Santa's sleigh!
It isn't fair, I've only *one* day,
It's about time, I should say,
Everybody found a way
To let *me* share in *their* Birthday!'

Pantomime Talk

Mum said to me
she'd take me to see
Jack and the Beanstalk one day.
Well, it was quite a good plot
Jack talked a lot
but the Beans had nothing to say.

****

Was Little Red Riding Hood not very bright
or her Grandmother's cottage exceedingly
shady?
Even allowing for poor eyesight
you'd think commonsense
would know the difference
between a Wolf and a little old lady.

Pantomime Talk

The Queen of Hearts
she baked some tarts
for the family on Christmas Day.
But the Knave of Hearts
stole half of those tarts
on a royal silver tray.
He then took the tarts
to the "Royal College of Crafty Arts"
and said 'Sell those tarts
at your next Sale of Arts
for whatever people will pay.
We'll share equal parts
of what you get for the tarts -
but, if you don't mind - I'll hang on to the tray!'

A Christmas Cracker

I'm a Christmas Cracker
Dressed for the occasion.
Gaudy, sparkly, eye-smacker
Primed for a sensation.
Laid out on the festive table
beaming bold temptations
for those unprepared, unable
to contain impatience.
Suddenly I'm taken
unceremoniously in hand,
lifted aloft and shaken
to invite another's hand.
Oh! The thrilling anticipation
of causing minds and strengths,
to focus concentration
on stretching me to lengths
of record breaking designation.
Until, 'Bang!' then I've exploded,
and gained a standing ovation!
My gems are all unloaded
to cries of sheer delight,
Cherished, to remember
what happened on a night
at a party in December,
when *I* was the Christmas Cracker
producer of the treasures.
The gaudy, sparkly, eye-smacker,
they'll remember as, "Most Precious."
They will, they will, *they will*.

Santa's Getting Old

All they need to do now, is Click,
and there they go, Click, Click, Click,
roaming through stores and stocks,
checking out the latest craze,
deciding what they want for Christmas.
Click, make sure its the right colour,
Click, to view from every angle,
Click, what size?
Click, how? Where? And of what is it made?
If a request was sent up the chimney
to me, today, like as not
I wouldn't know what it was,
or where to look for it, and
it would probably be the wrong model anyway.
The fun's gone out of it all.
I used to enjoy watching their dreams,
dolls and animals walking and talking with them,
castles with turrets reaching to the sky,
a cloak to transform them into
a proud Queen or brave Captain.
And I delivered their dreams.
They'd set up their castles,
don their cloaks and fairy wings
to swagger through Great Halls,

or flutter in and out of flower cups.
They could do that then,
because the expected toys,
when they arrived on Christmas Day
brought their magic with them.
Now they know exactly
what it is they are getting.
No surprises,
no dreams,
Just Click.

Ah well, - there are still
some stockings to fill.
...I don't do pillow cases,
I leave those to somebody else.

Sleeping Beauty

The King and Queen in their magnificent castle
were giving their servants no end of a hassle.
They were in the middle of preparations
for their baby's 'Naming Day' celebrations.
Everything must be polished, gleaming,
sparkling, shining…
The King shouted at the Queen, 'Stop that
nagging and whining.'
The Queen replied, 'Just buzz off and write the
invitations,
we don't need you adding to our botherations.'
So he went to his office, brought out his special
purple ink
and, for the next few days hardly slept a wink,
writing more than one thousand invitations
to all the posh and rich people - and some of his
relations.
On 'The Day', in a dining room twice as big as a
football pitch,
(*You realise of course they were terrifically rich*)
tables, with crystal goblets, gold plates and
cutlery were laid,
and delicious, sumptuous, luscious food
displayed.

Guests rushed to the tables to sit on the golden
chairs,
without even checking which places were theirs!
They gobbled and slurped, reaching over each
other to grab,
diving across the table with a fork to make a stab.
When guests were all belching, showing they'd
eaten their fill,
musicians sounded a fanfare - Everybody sat
quiet and still.
In through the windows, to everyone's surprise,
flew six fairy godmothers, like beautiful
butterflies.
Circling twice round the room to ensure they
were seen,
before coming gracefully to rest round the
King and Queen.
The First Fairy Godmother rose to claim her
duty;
waving her wand over the baby, 'I name thee,
Beauty.'
Four other Fairy Godmothers, in turn, each
waved her wand
to bestow upon the baby the blessing she'd
planned -

'Fashion Queen' 'Pop Star' 'Clever Clogs' 'Hip Dancer'...

SCREAMS rent the air!

Some guests leapt to their feet, others turned to stare,

as an enormous bluebottle floated round the room.

Twice the size of a fairy godmother, going Zoom, Zoom, Zoom.

Swooping over the guests. Some hid under tables, others ran around

bumping each other, knocking things over. Then came the sound

of an ear splitting *whistle*, and a booming voice bawled, 'SIT DOWN!' They all sat. Seemed no other choice.

'I am Chief Fairy Godmother and command respect!

I have been insulted, so I attend this Celebration as ***an insect***!

I, Chief Fairy Godmother, **UNINVITED!** *What* could be worse?

Therefore, I come not with a gift for the baby, but with a ***curse***!'

Gasps of horror as the creature chanted, waving a
great ugly wand,
'Princess Beauty on her seventeenth birthday
shall prick her hand
on a spindle, and from that SHE SHALL DIE!'
The voices of everyone in the Hall rose
in one great soaring cry.
A small explosion burst as the Chief Fairy
Godmother departed,
leaving behind an obnoxious smell, to prove
she'd farted.
Through the shouting and wailing and disarray,
a voice called '*SHUT UP! I've something*
important to say!
I am the **Sixth** *Fairy Godmother, and you've all*
forgotten
that I missed my turn because that rotten
creature shoved in and gave a wicked spell.
If I took my turn now, I just might well
save Princess Beauty from her fate.
So keep quiet, give me space - and wait.'
After a while she picked up her wand and,
addressing

the King and Queen, *'Now I'm ready to give my blessing.*
Princess Beauty, on her seventeenth
birthday, shall not die.
Instead, for one hundred years she shall lie
deeply asleep. BUT a Prince may instantly wake her with a kiss
to be married into a life of bliss.'
'So *that's* all right then,' they all said, 'she'll not have to lay
there fast asleep for more than half a day,
before a Prince comes along to claim his kiss.
So there's no need to worry any more, about any of this.'
So nobody did! When her seventeenth birthday dawned,
Princess Beauty knew nothing of the curse, never been warned.
She'd grown up to be a spoilt brat, given all her own way.
Told she was blessed and would marry a Prince one day.
Her Seventeenth Birthday Party and the old

guests, were boring.

So, as she'd never been all round the castle, went
exploring.

The huge castle was mysterious and exciting,
it seemed to her that distant turrets were inviting
her to cross courtyards where rooms were small,
and cosy.

Opening a door she saw a little old lady sweet
and rosy.

She entered. A spindle caught her hand. Blood
streamed.

The old lady dragged her to another room and
screamed,

'BEAUTY! SPINDLE! Servants rushed to help,
just in time

to lay Beauty on a sofa. Silence fell. Brambles
began to climb.

The Sixth Fairy Godmother, had *no idea* that the
original spell

included everyone in the castle, and that

all would be hidden well

out of sight under towering thorns and creepers,

and nothing more heard from the hundreds of
sleepers!

Of course, from time to time a Prince would
force a way
through the thickets to find where the Sleeping
Beauty lay.
The princely youth, braving the growls, snarls,
and roars,
of wild animals echoing up and down the
corridors,
prayed to be in time to save her from their cruel
jaws.
Gripping his sword, preparing himself to die in
her cause,
flung himself into the room - stopped - stared -
and fled!
Crying 'OH NO! Terrible! Horrible! Would
rather she were dead!'
And the Prince ran madly away, as had other
brave Princes before.
A shepherd boy, rambling by, watched as a
Prince tore
from the brambles, leapt his steed and galloped
over the horizon.
The boy smiled and, with an eager thought,
turned his eyes on

the thorny forest, murmuring, 'Maybe the old
stories are true.'
Gripping his stout cudgel, he beat his way
through
to the castle and entered, surprised to find a wide
open door
 and people sleeping, in chairs, against the wall,
and on the floor.
Roaring echoes of animals told him he might be
too late
to save Sleeping Beauty from a cruel fate.
But he was young and strong and for
many a year
had dealt with wild animals. So, without fear
entered the room. The sight of her beautiful face
drew him to her side, ignoring the horror and,
with noble grace,
knelt and kissed her. Opening her eyes of deepest
blue,
Beauty said, 'Hello, I've just been dreaming
about you.
My Prince! We'll be married and you'll have to
do what I say.'
He said 'Nope. Not a Prince. A shepherd. But

we'll marry anyway.

There's not one Prince would marry *you*. But
there's no need to weep...'

'Why no Prince?' she sobbed, 'What's your deal
with the sheep? '

'I promise to remain your ever faithful and
adoring lover.

Unlike Princes, I am tough and strong and
easily recover

from any shock. You may find my sheep
deadly boring,

but my life with them has inured me, and ensured
me capable of enduring

that booming, horrendously sickening, snarling
racket you make with **your snoring!**

Sleeping Beauty

Hayley Davey

Beauty and the Beast

A fearsome monster stalked the countryside,
people for miles around were terrified.
When he sharpened teeth and claws on rocks and
stones,
they imagined him chewing up their bones.
Through walls of steel his horns could penetrate,
and his claws dig up a housing estate.
He could lasso a man with his long, long tail,
lift, and fling him to a faraway Dale.
Each time he shook his long, shaggy hair
a rotten stench poisoned the country air.
People rang their council to complain,
councillors discussed complaints again and
again,
but none of them had any idea what to do,
until up spoke a new woman councillor, who
asked, 'Does anyone know *why* the beast is so
cross?'
Roars of laughter shook the chamber up down
and across.
She ignored the discourtesy and, at the end of the
day
went to visit an old wise woman, for what *she*
might say;

hoping a hundred and fifty years experience
might tell
of an old simple remedy. The old woman said
'Well…
in the olden days, any local Beauty
would consider it to be her pride and duty
to kiss the Beast and make him into a Prince,
but these days young Beauties are hard to
convince.
So the poor Beast believed he'd receive Beauty's
kiss
and they'd both be transported to a life of bliss.
Now, he's finding it most aggravating
to be kept hanging about for such a long time,
waiting.'
'I understand,' said the counsellor, 'but
please tell me *how*
to persuade a Beauty to kiss the Beast NOW!'
'Advertise! Offer celebrity status and untold
riches!
Unfortunately resources have rather dwindled for
witches.'
The councillor heard this, knowing if she had no
success

before the next council meeting, she'd be in a right mess.

She looked in the mirror that stood on her shelf and asked, 'Should I try kissing the Beast myself?'

The mirror replied, 'You should ask if that old twaddle is true,

because if you kiss the Beast and it isn't, then what'll you do?'

'Well I suppose I'd be eaten or collapse from the stink.

Yes, there *are* fates worse than death I think.'

Just then the doorbell rang and there, to her great surprise,

stood the most beautiful girl in the world before her very eyes!

'My name is Sumerilla, I saw your advert, hope I'm not too late.'

'Ye-es, NO! Come in, come in, we'll arrange a date.'

And, told her of benefits to be won by kissing the Beast,

Sumerilla said, 'Status and riches do not interest me in the least.'

'Then why do you want to kiss the Beast, a
lovely girl like you?'
'That's my secret,' said Sumerilla, 'but I'm not
telling you.
However, there are one or two items I require to
be met,
a large bottle of my favourite perfume, and a
brush and comb set.
I'll come back in the morning, no need to be
rushed.'
'You may have anything in the world you want.'
the councillor gushed.
She bought a huge bottle of Sumerilla's perfume,
costing the earth,
and hairbrushes, silver backed to show off their
worth.
When Sumerilla returned, the councillor told her
she was brave,
gave her the perfume and brushes, and saw her
off with a wave.
Sumerilla, walking quickly, soon was well on her
way.
Whenever she caught a whiff of the Beast, gave a
hefty spray

of her lovely perfume to make her way clear.
After a while she knew he was near.
And there, as she rounded the side of the hill,
saw him close by, lying quite still.
She thought, 'He looks like a pile of shabby old
rugs,
hardly a beguiling allurement for rapturous
hugs!'
At that moment the Beast rose to his feet and
bowed,
Sumerilla gasped, wondering had she spoken her
thoughts aloud?
'Good morning Beast, I'm charmed to be greeted
in such style. Now, may I request you to be
seated?
I'm sure you'll agree we have a lot to talk about,
but that will be difficult if I have to shout.'
The Beast immediately crouched nearer the
ground.
'I do hope you don't mind me waving this
perfume around,
but you have rather been neglecting your hair,
so, if you will please sit quietly there,
while I brush and comb you a

wickedly fashionable re-style,
I'll describe to you, our bewitchingly,
spellbinding, future lifestyle.
So she did.
Then warned him, 'Before you say a word,
remember to whisper, or you'll be heard
by everybody, in all directions, for miles.'
The Beast whispered, Sumerilla's face lit up with
smiles.
She asked the Beast to lift her up high
she wanted to whisper something but she was
shy.
The Beast lifted her up close to his ear.
She whispered, 'I don't want to marry a Prince
my dear,
so, instead of *me* kissing *you,* would it be alright
if I asked you to give me a little love bite?'
The Beast obliged most happily
and, to their delight, quite snappily,
Sumerilla grew to enormous size.
Now they could gaze into each others eyes.
Then she became beautifully, glossily hirsute,
and, with horns, tail and claws looked fetchingly
cute.

They snuggled together in utter bliss,
now she could safely give him a kiss.
They went to the Town Hall the very next day,
for Councillors to hear what they had to say.
'*Listen* to the proposition we put to you.
No, *don't* run away, show good manners, *do!*
Though we both are armed with horns, claws and
tail,
we promise our good nature will ever prevail,
on condition you keep us well supplied
with the perfume favoured by my bride.
And all of you, Her impeccable taste will
convince,
a noble Beast, in grandeur, exceeds any Prince.'

Goldilocks and The Three Bears

A little vandal
broke into a cottage
and gobbled up all
of the little one's porridge.
Then rampaged about,
quite unawares
that this dear little cottage
belonged to Three Bears,
who'd gone for a walk
in the bluebell wood,
to work up a relish
for their breakfast food.
After romping around,
she broke one of the chairs,
then had the cheek
to go running upstairs!
There she found chocolate
and coca cola,
gobbled and guzzled
spilling them over,
as she jumped up and down
on all the beds,
making a terrible mess
on the covers and spreads.

Then the little vandal
not caring a jot,
snuggled down
in the little one's cot
and, closing her eyes
fell fast off to sleep.
So *she* never heard
the little one weep,
when Mummy and Daddy
brought him back to the cottage
to find someone
had eaten his porridge.
'Oh look, they've broken
my lovely chair!'
He broke into wails
and cries of despair,
putting Mummy and Daddy
in a furious rage.
'How dare someone
break in and rampage
while we are out!
Hark! That sounds quite near,
someone is hiding
somewhere in here!'

Goldilocks and the Three Bears

So they crept upstairs
to follow the sound
of noisy snores,
and the culprit was found!
The Three Bears growled
and ran to the bed,
Goldilocks screamed
and, dodging them, fled
out of the house
and ran far away.
That was when Mummy
was then heard to say,
'I wouldn't have minded,
but when *She* accused
Us of frightening *Her,*
I was not amused.
She'll tell *such* a tale,
and the story will spread.
Now what am I like?
Like *a bear with a sore head.'*

Mother Goose

Mother Goose, and her son Jack,
owned a large goose that flew there and back
for many a mile without ever stopping.
When Mother Goose required to go shopping
Goose would fly her there upon its broad back
but would fly no one else, not even Jack.
That's how Mother Goose came by her name.
When she was seen overhead folk would
exclaim,
'There goes Mother Goose flying to the shops,
better get out of the way before that Goose plop,
plops!'
Children looked up with giggles and snickers
to see Mother Goose's big flowery knickers.
Jack bought *himself* a goose one day at the fair,
explained, 'The choice was either the goose or a
bear.
Maybe my goose will never give me rides on her
back,
but at least I won't be scared when she's
looking for a snack.'
The goose waddled home beside him, chatting on
the way
about world affairs and the price of hay.

'This is Priscilla,' announced Jack, 'and she belongs to me.'
Mother Goose and Goose swept a curtsey from the knee,
'Welcome,' they greeted, 'Hang your bonnet on the peg.'
Next morning Priscilla gave Jack a golden egg.
Jack rushed to Mother Goose, 'See what Priscilla laid for me.'
'It looks like gold all through,' said she,
'We'll take it to the merchant for money we can spend,
be a change from us asking how much will he lend!'
The merchant dealt them so much money in a sack,
Goose declared, 'Can't carry *you* with that lot on my back.'
So Mother Goose walked home with a hop-skip-and-dance,
singing all the way of Jack's lucky game of chance.
When Jack arrived home, he rushed with the sack to show Priscilla the money Goose had brought back.

Then took her shopping to buy all she wished for
herself.
They looked all around, then high on a shelf
Priscilla spied a beautiful blue bonnet
with yellow flowers embroidered on it.
That's all she wanted, she insisted, 'Nothing
more,'
but suggested Mother Goose should buy from the
store
all *she* wanted. So, Mother Goose the very next
day,
ordered a fashionably, fabulous, tremendous
array
of garments from the store, and, in a short while,
Mother Goose, *every day*, wore a different style.
She was fat and bouncy, her smile wide as an
oven dish.
She loved bright colours and frilly skirts she
could swish.
She presented herself at all the important places,
Grand Balls, Fashion Shows and, of course, The
Races.
But someone else, always present at those events,
- Grand Duke Greedybucket - noted her
extravagance.

He used spies and bribes, and, following the
clues,
discovered from whence came the riches of
Mother Goose.
He swore by the bones in his Grandfather's legs
to own the 'Goose that laid the Golden Eggs'.
He sent out his men with the strict instruction,
'Make sure you manage the secret abduction
of the goose that lays only eggs of gold,
then I shall, forever, enjoy riches untold!'
Priscilla's disappearance caused great
consternation,
Mother Goose sobbing and wailing in loud
lamentation.
Goose announced, 'She's been kidnapped I think,
so straight away we must look for the link.
 You go around and question everybody, Jack,
I'll fly in search, with Mother Goose, then report
back.'
Jack chatted and questioned everyone he met,
when they heard about Priscilla they were most
upset.
'Nobody in our village or town would snatch and
carry her off,

you mark our words and go looking for a *toff.*'
Goose, flying in search, saw a man walking
with a goose beside.
'No other goose wears a blue bonnet!' Goose
cried.
Mother Goose immediately leapt from Goose's
back
and landed right on top of the man, flat! smack!
Down he went bang on his bum
with a noise like a booming kettledrum,
attracting stares from anyone near,
but what had happened was not quite clear.
The unfortunate man, hidden from sight,
kicked and struggled and yelled in fright.
Mother Goose, sitting, her skirts spreading wide,
showed two extra legs kicking out from inside!
Folk gaped as she seemed to be blobbing like a
jelly,
with a voice bellowing out, from the middle of
her belly!
Jack returned, in time to help Mother Goose to
rise.
Everyone doubled up laughing in surprise
as Mother Goose stood up, and swept her skirts
aside,

to reveal Grand Duke Greedybucket crouching, mortified
that everyone should see this outrageous harassment
by Mother Goose, as he squirmed with embarrassment.
Priscilla tried to move forward, so glad to see Jack again.
Jack shouted in furious indignation, 'LOOK!
PRISCILLA'S HELD ON A CHAIN!'
Gasps of horror from the people, all of them shocked
to see a chain twisted round Priscilla's neck and tightly locked.
Jack grabbed clippers from someone and cut her free,
then he furiously turned on the Duke, who cried *'It wasn't mee!'*
'CLEAR OFF!' yelled Jack, stroking Priscilla's neck, to ease the bruise,
*'**And drag your filthy chain with you, before I make it a noose**!'*
Goose, with wide stretched wings chased the Duke far away,

then told them, 'He'll not return in a thousand
years and a day.'
When Mother Goose heard this, she immediately,
just for a lark,
bought Grand Duke Greedybucket's Castle and
Park.
Children came in every day to have fun,
adventures and happy, happy times,
While Mother Goose sat in the castle writing
Fairy Tales and Nursery Rhymes.

Mother Christmas

Hi! This is Mother Christmas talking,
and I've rather more to say than "HO, HO, HO"
If I can make myself heard above the squawking
of our brood, mouths wide open fortissimo.
It's alright for him, he has the reindeer team
and they can *fly* for heaven's sake,
while I'm left paddling a leaky canoe upstream,
or driving down a mountain side on a faulty
brake.
Right now I'm here, waiting for him to land,
the warehouse packed to the roof and up to the
doors.
It's galling to have to make out he's a one man
band,
who do they think does the organising and gritty
chores?
Good thing 'Powers That Be' grant us 'Time'.
the kiddies all think he does it by magic of
course
can't let on we use wormholes through
space, and 'Untime.'
It'd spoil it for them to know we use a scientific
source.
I just wish he'd make us into a proper
partnership,

Mother Christmas

I'd love a chance to take a turn driving the team
and sleigh.

He thinks I couldn't manage the reindeer, haven't
the grip.

Well, it's likely *he'll* not be driving them much
longer anyway.

I'm talking now about global warming, you
know,

I don't think it's even crossed his mind,

but what use is a reindeer sleigh without the
snow?

When the change comes I don't intend to be left
behind,

I've been training up a team of camel calves,

ready for when we have to drive over

desert sand.

He'll see then I don't do things by halves!

I'm keeping this strictly to myself you
understand.

I've invented a snazzy coach called a 'Camel
Tote'.

Comfy, shady, lots of room and the harness will
lift it

right up in the air, so when we move off it'll
float!

Mother Christmas

Musn't forget the Space-Time-Drive, *he'll* have
to shift it
from *his* reindeer sleigh to *my* Camel Tote -
that's for when I need to whiz into Space.
And here's another thing might cause dispute,
bright red and fluffy white will be distinctly out
of place.
Something more dignified - a gold lame trouser
suit?
Something for the head, again I shall rebel
I mean to say - *pulease* spare me the *hood.*
I'm thinking more tiara, - a circlet of stars would
look well.
There! That's Camel Team, Tote, dress and
headgear. Good.
Glad that's settled, it's been brewing for ages.
I know I must seem selfish, but I don't care,
I'm a hard working woman, no time to myself,
no wages.
Now, when the time comes I know I shall dare
to drive my Team and Tote into Space - and the
stars will smile.
And I'll have a great big grin on my face
delivering the children's gifts in such style!

Mother Christmas

They'll love all the glitter and gold,
and the Tote and the lovely little Camel Team.
There. A wonderful secret you've just been told!
So keep all this to yourself ...
Mother Christmas's Dream.

Cinderella - the true story.

Cinderella was a pain in the neck
driving her step sisters mad,
trailing around dressed like a wreck
looking hard done by and sad.
Especially when visitors were there
to whisper, 'What a shame,
she does all the work, it isn't fair.'
and the family got a bad name.
When came the time for the Palace Ball
she sighed to her sisters, 'Go, enjoy,
I have nothing to wear at all,
I'll just stay here with the scullery boy.'
Her sisters cried, 'They'll all be asking where
you are,
we'll get dirty looks all night,
they'll say we're both too jealous by far
and locked you in out of spite.'
After they left, she called to the boy,
smiled, and said, 'Shall we dance?'
The poor boy's face lit up with joy
believing this to be true romance.
Their little dance had barely begun,
Whiz! Bang! Now look whose appeared!
Fairy Godmother like a shot from a gun!

Cinderella

Said the boy, 'That woman is weird!'
Cinderella replied, 'She's not weird at all,
she's smart, she's clever, she's cool.
No one will recognise me at the Ball,
everyone there I shall fool.
I wanted you here, boy, so you could see
how she makes with the wand and a wink.
Come on Godmother, "**One, Two, Threee!**"
There now, what do you think?'
Cinderella stood in a beautiful gown
of shimmering satin and lace,
little glass slippers, a golden crown,
and a smug little smile on her face.
The scullery boy threw himself to his knees
and cried, 'I beg you do not leave,
Cinderella will you marry me, please?'
and wiped his nose on his sleeve.
'Get up, take your dirty hands off my dress!
I'd sooner marry a horse.
Anyone but a fool would guess
I shall marry the Prince, of course.'
Four white horses, a coach of gold,
horsemen, trappings, the lot!
Now, comes the truth of the tale we've been told,

when her Godmother declared, 'Here's the plot.
You'd better be back by Twelve o-Clock,
I must return these before dawn.
Otherwise we'll be up in the dock,
so don't say I didn't warn.'
Cinderella gasped, 'Do I understand
you've been and pinched all of these?
Why didn't you wave the wand in your hand
over mice, a pumpkin and fleas?'
'There is a limit to magic you know,'
said her Godmother, sounding aggrieved,
'Now step up inside and away you go,
no one will know they've been thieved.'
Cinderella's arrival at the ball
was an instant dazzling success,
introduced as '*Lady Conningthemall*'.
Everyone gasped, 'What beauty! What elegance!
That dress!'
The Prince stepped forward to kiss her hand,
'You shall lead the dance with me.'
The music struck up at his command,
everyone crowded to see
Prince Charming dance with the beautiful girl
whom nobody knew at all,

and all were caught in the dizzying whirl
of excitement around the Great Hall.
The stepsisters looked at each other and laughed,
'She's the spitting image!' they said.
'Nah, *can't* be her, don't be daft,
we know she's at home in bed.'
Cinderella danced in the Prince's arms,
she was having the time of her life,
she knew he was falling for her charms
and would ask her to be his wife.
She heard the clock strike the Midnight Hour
and cried, 'I must go! I'm late!'
The Prince's looks of love turned sour,
'How *dare* you go off on another date!'
The Prince held tightly to her arm,
she freed herself and fled.
He could be heard shouting, 'Sound the alarm!'
as out of the Palace she sped.
The coach was waiting by the gate,
it's doors were open wide,
'YOU STUPID GIRL! I said don't be late!'
and her Godmother dragged her inside.
Then yelled to the coachman 'Go! Go! Go!
we haven't a moment to lose!'

Cinderella

Cinderella felt a draught round her toe,
and saw she'd lost one of her shoes.
Coach, horses, returned before dawn
and the coachmen paid off with a threat -
'Not a *word!*, or you'll wish you'd never been
born!'
That brought *them* all out in a sweat.
The very next day it was headline news,
'TROOPS OF SOLDIERS OUT ON A SEARCH
FOR WICKED GIRL WHO LOST ONE OF
HER SHOES
AFTER LEAVING OUR PRINCE IN THE
LURCH."
So she went into hiding and spent her time,
(Though I wouldn't swear this on the bible)
writing a best selling Pantomime,
and her Godmother sued her for libel.

Mary, Mary, Quite Contrary.

Mary, Mary,
Was contrary,
Preparing for a local Garden Show.
Horrible smells
From the cockle shells,
And mussels and oysters she was hoping to grow.

Flinging fish oil
To compost the soil,
Sent out whiffs as if from a take-away!
Cats ran for miles
With Cheshire Cat smiles,
Believing this must be *their* 'Happy Fishness
Day.'

Silver bells
Among the shells,
(While cats pounced around looking for fish)
Rang charming chimes
Of Nursery Rhymes,
Seeming to promise - 'Here, you'll find your
dearest wish'

Mary, Mary, Quite Contrary

Folk came from miles
With hopeful smiles
For a promising day of delights.
Fish and cats
Put stop to all thats
With the biggest and blackest of blights.

Stopped in their tracks,
Folk turned their backs,
Before they'd even heard the first cat, 'Miaow.'
And, I'm afraid,
Not one pretty maid,
But angry folk, in a big blazing row.

A few notes about the author and her poems.

Hazel Rennie was born 1927 and brought up in a West Yorkshire village on the edge of the moors.

Hazel looks down the long years to her early childhood, gathering along the way, fragments of remembered conversations to weave into poems describing traditions such as 'Bringing in the Yule' and the making of a 'mistletoe bough'.

Her personal memories of 'going a-mumming' bring pictures of the children dressing up; Hazel wore an old jacket of Uncle John's, reaching down to her ankles, and his flat cap. Sometimes they blacked their faces.

In 'Us Mummers' the offer to 'Scrub yer stones' means scrub the front doorstep with white or yellow scouring stone. 'Click on t' bones' involved our village butcher in providing a couple of suitably shaped bones, well scraped of meat, which the children then took home to scrub until the bones were smooth and gleaming. These they clicked between their fingers like castanets, providing rhythm for singers and dancers.

Although Hazel ends 'Us Mummers' with 'We only asket a penny int' basket etc.' this can be put down to 'poet's licence' because she doesn't remember any of them *asking* for money, though they invariably came away with a satisfying bag of Christmas goodies.

Actually, Mummers went round on New Year's Eve and sometimes Hallowe'en.